The Other Sisters

I Talk You Talk Press

Old Secrets – Modern Mysteries Book 5

CONTENTS

THE OTHER SISTERS CHARACTER LIST

James Winchester was a diplomat for twenty years. Before that, he worked for the British Secret Service. He is married to Sarah, and they live in Hill House in western Scotland.

Sarah Winchester is a retired schoolteacher. She grew up in Scotland.

James and Sarah fell in love when they were students in Paris. James disappeared, and Sarah returned to Scotland. Forty years later, they met again.

You can read more about James' and Sarah's recent lives in books one, two, three and four of the Old Secrets - Modern Mysteries series: The Blue Lace Curtain, End House, On the Run and Killer.

Anna Berryman is James' daughter. She didn't know anything about James until after her Aunt Maggie died.

Elizabeth Berryman is Anna's mother. She was a doctor. She met James Winchester in Cambodia. He said his name was Peter Bridges.

Miriam Berryman is Elizabeth's daughter and Anna's half-sister. She is also called Besjana.

Vjosa is one of James' contacts. He has useful information.

Other characters:

Miles is Anna's boyfriend.

Andy is James' nephew. He works at a university in Italy.

Carim Aldaman was Elizabeth Berryman's husband and Miriam's father.

Majlinda Luan Gegaj was Miriam's nurse. She escaped from the Kosovo war and took Miriam to Albania.

Len and Fiona own the hotel in Beautore, the village where James and Sarah live.

1. THE DAY AFTER THE FUNERAL

It was the day after the funeral. Anna was emptying the house. It was rented, and the owner wanted it back as soon as possible.

She was upstairs packing Maggie's' clothes into boxes to send to the charity shop, when one of the removal men called out to her.

"Excuse me, Miss. Can you come down and tell us what we should do with this cabinet?"

Anna ran down the stairs. Almost everything in the house was going to the charity shop, but some of the bigger pieces of furniture were going to be sold at auction.

The removal man was standing in the living room. He pointed to the big wooden cabinet in the corner.

"Is this for the charity shop or for the auction?" he asked.

"Isn't it part of the house?" asked Anna.

"No. It's been there a long time, but it isn't built into the house."

Anna looked at it. "I don't know," she said.

"Why don't you keep it?" said the removal man. "It's a nice piece of furniture."

Anna looked at it again. It was old and made of dark wood. She didn't want it in her modern apartment. "Auction, please," she said.

"OK Miss, we'll move it now. Do you want these armchairs to go to the auction too?"

"No, I'm giving them to the charity shop."

"OK. This cabinet's the last piece of furniture. We'll put it in the truck, and we'll go."

"Thank you," said Anna. "Your company will send the bill to me in Birmingham?"

"Yes, Miss. We know what to do. Do you want help with all those boxes upstairs? The ones for the charity shop?"

"No, thank you. I'm leaving a key here. Some volunteers from the charity will come tomorrow and take them away."

"OK."

The removal men had a hard time moving the cabinet, but finally they got it outside the small terraced house, and into their big truck.

When the removal men had gone, Anna went into the living room to clean. She was surprised to see that there was a small door in the wall behind where the cabinet had been.

She opened it. It was a small cupboard. Inside, there were a few school notebooks, some old jigsaw puzzles and a photograph album.

This is strange, she thought. *That big old cabinet was in this corner for as long as I can remember. I guess someone forgot to empty this cupboard.*

She took out the notebooks and album, and she sat on the floor to look at them.

She stared at the notebooks. Some had "Margaret Berryman" written on the covers, but others had "Elizabeth Berryman" on the cover. Maggie's real name was Margaret, but her parents called her Maggie, thought Anna. But who was Elizabeth?

Anna looked through the notebooks. Some pages had dates on them. It seemed that Elizabeth was about two years younger than Maggie. There were notebooks from high school for Maggie, but none for Elizabeth. *She must have been a sister. Maybe she died,* thought Anna. *I wonder why no one ever told me.*

She put the notebooks on the floor, and opened the photograph album. Yes, there was a sister. Anna looked at photographs of a little girl in a party dress. The girl was sitting in an armchair holding a baby. The armchair was one of the two that Anna planned to send to the charity shop. *So I guess that's Maggie and Elizabeth,* thought Anna. She looked at the few photographs of the two girls together - Christmas Day, a birthday party for Maggie, summer holidays... There were many photographs of Maggie, but not many of Elizabeth.

"When's the funeral?" Anna jumped up. A woman was standing in the doorway of the living room.

"When's the funeral?" the woman asked again.

"It was yesterday. Who are you?" asked Anna.

"Someone who knew Maggie a long time ago," answered the

woman. "But I don't know who you are."

"I'm Anna Berryman.

Anna was not frightened, but she felt angry.

The woman threw a backpack on the floor, and sat down in one of the armchairs. Anna sat in the other armchair and stared at the strange visitor.

The woman was about sixty. Her hair was grey. Her skin was tanned and lined. It looked as if she spent a lot of time outdoors. The backs of her hands had scars on them. She was wearing jeans and a T-shirt, big wooden and copper earrings, and a matching necklace. The backpack on the floor was old and dirty. Anna didn't know what to think of her.

The woman was staring back at Anna. "You look like your father," she said.

Anna was amazed. "You know what my father looked like?"

The woman looked surprised. "Of course. It was more than thirty years ago, but I remember."

She paused and smiled. Anna saw that she had very beautiful, bright blue eyes.

"Sorry, you don't know me. I'm Elizabeth," said the woman.

"You're Maggie's sister. I have only just found out about you. Of course you would know Maggie's boyfriend."

Elizabeth said nothing. She sat and looked at Anna for a few moments. Then she stood up and went to the window.

"I always hated this room. It was so small and dark. It seemed like a prison to me. I wanted to escape. The last time I was in this room was thirty-three years ago. I was pregnant."

She turned back and smiled at Anna. "I'm your mother. But I called you Ayesha, not Anna."

"No! That's not true!" Anna shouted.

2. AN OLD STORY

Elizabeth came back, and sat down again in the chair facing Anna. She reached out to take Anna's hand, but Anna moved her hand away.

"Tell me what you know," said Elizabeth quietly. "What did they tell you?"

Anna couldn't say anything. Maggie had been cheerful, dark-haired and pretty. The woman sitting opposite her was thin. She looked tough. Anna wondered if she had been a soldier.

Elizabeth tried again. "I'm sorry. You've had a shock. Why don't we go to the pub and talk about it there?"

"My grandparents never drank alcohol. Maggie didn't, and I don't either. Most of the house is packed up, but I can make a cup of tea," said Anna.

When Anna came back from the kitchen, Elizabeth was looking at the notebooks. Anna gave Elizabeth a cup of tea and sat down. "I don't believe you. I don't understand anything. Tell me everything."

Elizabeth drank some tea and frowned. "I hate English tea. OK, I'll tell you the whole story. But first, please tell me what you know. It will make it easier."

Anna took a deep breath. She never talked to anyone about her life. Now she had a chance to tell someone.

"I grew up in this house with two old people. I called them Mum and Dad. They said they had adopted me. I asked about my real mother and father, but they always said they didn't know anything. Maggie was my much, much older sister. She was more like my mother, but I called her Maggie. Then I found out that Maggie was really my mother."

"How did you find out?" Elizabeth's voice was gentle.

"My high school had school trips. Once my class went to Paris for three days, and another time, they went to Germany. I was never allowed to go. Then, when I was sixteen, Mum and Dad died. After that, there was just Maggie and me. It was my last year at school, and my last chance to go on a school trip. I thought Maggie would say I couldn't go. I was always a very good child, but this time I decided I was going on the trip, and no one would stop me!"

"Good for you!" Elizabeth smiled.

"I needed a passport. I was sixteen, so I could apply for one without permission from my family. I went to get my birth certificate, and that's when I found out. I was born in Scotland and my mother's name was Margaret Berryman. It said, 'father unknown'."

"What did you think?" asked Elizabeth.

"I thought that everything made sense. The people I called Mum and Dad were old when I was born. I never understood why they adopted a baby. But then I thought I knew the story. Maggie got pregnant. She wasn't married, so she went to Scotland, and I was born there. Mum and Dad were really my grandparents. They told everyone that they had adopted me so people would not gossip about Maggie. But Maggie was my real mother."

"Did you talk to Maggie about it?"

"I tried. I told her I had seen my birth certificate. I asked her to tell me about my father. She got very upset. She said that things were very complicated. She said that I was only sixteen. She would tell me when I was older."

"Did you go on the school trip?"

"Yes. We went to Belgium. I didn't enjoy it."

"And you never asked Maggie again?"

"No. Maggie was my real mother, even if she had pretended to be my sister. I loved her very much. It didn't matter that I never knew about my father."

Elizabeth looked very sad. "I loved Maggie too. Do you want to know the true story?"

Anna wasn't sure. She didn't like this woman. "Maggie was my mother. You can't change that."

"You are right. Maggie was your mother in most ways, but I want you to know the truth. I thought Maggie would tell you. I will tell you the story of two little girls."

3. TWO LITTLE GIRLS

"Once upon a time, there were two little girls. They were sisters. The older girl's name was Margaret. Everyone called her Maggie. She was a very cheerful, pretty girl. Her parents loved her very much.

"The second sister's name was Elizabeth. The parents tried to call her Betty, but Elizabeth didn't like that name. She would never listen, or answer if anyone called her Betty. She was different. Her parents tried very hard. They loved her, but they didn't like her very much."

"That must have been terrible for you," said Anna.

Elizabeth smiled. "No. You must understand. I didn't do anything to help them to like me. I loved my parents, but I didn't like them. Maggie was special. We shared a bedroom. We were very different, but we were good friends. I wanted to escape from this house. I wanted to escape from this life. I hated it. Our parents wanted us to leave school, get a job, get married, have children."

"But that's normal," said Anna. "That's what every young girl wants to do."

"I wanted something different. I wanted to leave this town and travel. I wanted to be another kind of person."

"I think you got what you wanted," said Anna. "How did you do it?"

"When Elizabeth was eleven, Maggie was thirteen. Maggie was average at school, but Elizabeth was very clever. Elizabeth's teacher said there were scholarships to boarding school for clever children. Elizabeth thought, I can escape! She wrote her father's signature on the application forms and she took the exams. She was lucky. She won a full scholarship to a boarding school in the south of England.

"Her parents couldn't stop her. Her sister, Maggie, was very upset. She loved her younger sister very much. But the younger sister was not a nice person. She knew she would miss Maggie, but this was her chance to escape. She went away to boarding school and almost never came home again."

"What about holidays?" asked Anna. She did not like Elizabeth's story, but she wanted to hear it to the end.

"Elizabeth made friends at the boarding school. She liked her friends' families more than she liked her own family. The friends' families invited her to stay with them. After boarding school, she won a scholarship to a medical university. She wanted to be a doctor. After she went to university she never visited her family. She missed Maggie, but her life was so exciting, she never tried to call her or to see her."

4. THE DREAM

Elizabeth stopped talking. She looked very tired, and her face was a strange grey colour.

"Are you OK?" asked Anna. "Shall I make more tea?"

"Do you have any coffee?" asked Elizabeth.

"There is instant coffee in the kitchen."

Elizabeth frowned. She leant down and opened the backpack. She pulled out a plastic bag of tea bags. "Could you make me tea with this? It's green tea. It's very good for you. And a glass of water would be nice."

Anna made tea using the tea bags.

She took the cups, and a glass of water back to the living room.

"Thank you." Elizabeth took the glass of water. She had some pills in her hand. She put them in her mouth and drank some water.

She drank some of the green tea and smiled. "That's better."

Anna drank some tea too. She thought the tea was terrible. It tasted like boiled grass.

Elizabeth looked much better. She started talking again.

"The summer before I finished medical school, I went to Cambodia for three months as a volunteer. The Pol Pot regime had just been defeated. There were so many people who needed help. It was very difficult, but I loved it. I knew that I wanted to be a doctor for international aid.

"I met a man there. He said his name was Peter Bridges. He said he was working for the Red Cross. I liked him a lot. I wasn't interested in a long-term relationship, but we had an affair. I was back in England, and studying for my final exams when I realized I was pregnant. I was going to have a baby. I didn't want any help from Peter Bridges, but I thought I should tell him about the baby. I contacted the Red Cross. They had never heard of him.

"I wanted to go to Asia again. I wanted to have a career as a doctor. So I came here. I asked my parents, your grandparents, if they would take the baby when it was born. They said 'no'. But Maggie argued. She wanted to take the baby. They discussed it a lot, and finally, they made a plan. Your grandfather was very angry. He said that the baby could come here, but he also said I must never come back to this house. I must never contact anyone in the family. I didn't want to agree, but I wanted to be a doctor and help people more."

"But why was Maggie's name on the birth certificate?" Anna was puzzled.

"That was very easy! I went to Scotland. I registered with a local doctor and a hospital. I used Maggie's name. I had Maggie's papers, and there was no photo ID then. Just before you were born, Maggie came up to Scotland and she said her name was Elizabeth.

"You were such a beautiful baby. I called you Ayesha, but Maggie said the name was too foreign. She wanted to call you Anna. I was very sad to give you up, but I wanted my dream more. Please understand that I was very young. Maggie took you from Scotland and brought you back to this house. As soon as I was strong enough, I got a job with an aid organization. I have been a doctor in many different countries. That has been my life."

Anna didn't have anything to say. It was all so strange and surprising. *All my life, my family has been lying to me,* she thought. She felt very angry.

"Why did you come back now?" she shouted. "Why did you tell me this story? I was OK before! I was sad that Maggie was dead, but now I know that my life was a lie!"

"I heard that Maggie was dead. I knew our parents were dead. I thought my promise was over. I could come. I wanted to go to Maggie's funeral. I wanted to say goodbye to her, and say I was sorry. But I was too late. How did she die?"

"It was a very unlucky accident," said Anna. "She worked at an insurance company. She walked out of the front door of the office building, and a speeding van driver lost control and drove up onto the footpath. The van hit Maggie, and she died immediately."

"Oh, poor Maggie." Elizabeth looked very sad.

Elizabeth looked around the room. "How about you? Where are you going to live now?"

"I left this house five years ago. I work in a bank in Birmingham. I have a nice apartment. I have a boyfriend. I am going back to Birmingham tonight. I have been emptying this house ever since I arrived."

"Are you happy, Anna?"

"Yes. I am very happy. I have a good life. But that's thanks to Maggie, not to you."

"Yes. That's true. But I hope you can understand, and I hope you can forgive me. Can you take some time off work, or maybe even leave your job? I am retired now. But I still have some things I want to do. You could come with me. Would you like to travel?"

"Why would I do that? I have a good life. Why would I change my life for you? I don't understand why you gave me away. I will never forgive you! You are a stranger. You are nothing to me."

"Well, I tried," said Elizabeth. She stood up and picked up her backpack. She handed Anna a business card. "If you change your mind, this is my address in Geneva. I have an apartment there. It's nice. Please think about coming to see me there."

Anna looked away. She didn't answer. Elizabeth touched her on the arm. "I loved you. I still love you. I'm sorry."

Anna heard her leave the house. She heard the door close. She tore the business card into very small pieces.

5. MILES

Anna's boyfriend was waiting at the station in Birmingham. He ran to her and hugged her. "Oh, my poor sweetheart. Did you have a bad time?"

"It wasn't easy. But I'm OK now."

"I'll take you home. You must be tired. When is everything from the house coming?" asked Miles.

"There isn't anything. I sent some of the furniture to the auction, I gave some things to charity, and I threw everything else away. Except for these."

Anna handed Miles two paper bags. Miles looked inside. He saw a few pictures, an album, and some old school notebooks. "Is that all you wanted to keep?"

"Yes." Anna was tired. They reached the car. She put her suitcase in the boot and Miles added the bags.

Anna wanted to go to her apartment. She didn't want to have a conversation, but Miles was talking.

"You'll get the money from the auction and the sale of the house, won't you?"

"Maybe I will get a few hundred pounds from the auction. But the house was rented."

"Oh." Miles stopped talking. He drove into the car park of Anna's building. He kissed her on the cheek. "Sleep well," he said.

Anna got out of the car. Miles opened the boot from inside the car, and Anna took her suitcase and bags out. She watched Miles drive away.

She walked to the entrance of the apartment building. She was carrying her suitcase and the heavy bags. Her back hurt and she had a headache. *I'll feel better once I'm inside,* she thought. *Why didn't I tell him about Elizabeth? I guess he wouldn't understand, and I don't want to think about it.*

Anna's apartment was in a new tower block. It was very light and modern. Anna loved it. Everything in the apartment was new. Everything matched. She was very happy to be back.

Over the next few days Anna often thought about Maggie. She was angry about the lies. She tried not to think about Elizabeth. Her birth mother had seemed so strange. *Imagine if she came to visit me here,* thought Anna, looking around her beautiful living room. *This apartment wouldn't suit her at all. And imagine what Miles would think of her. She was wearing jeans and she must be sixty years old! She has skin like a very old woman. That strange jewellery and she had a dirty backpack! Miles wouldn't like Elizabeth at all.*

She put the school notebooks and the photograph album in a cupboard and closed the door. *Forget about them,* she told herself. *You have a good life. You don't have to think about Elizabeth or your mystery father.*

At first, Anna was very tired, and she didn't worry when Miles didn't telephone her. After a week, Anna called him. "Sorry," he said. "I've been very busy. I'll call you next weekend."

Miles didn't call on Saturday. On Sunday, Anna went to eat lunch with a friend from work. Cynthia invited her to an expensive restaurant near the canal. "You've had a hard time," said Cynthia. "Come out with me. It will cheer you up."

They were enjoying their meal when Cynthia said, "Isn't that Miles over there?"

Anna looked across the restaurant. Miles was sitting at a table with a very pretty blonde girl. He was leaning across the table and holding her hands.

"I thought he was your boyfriend," said Cynthia.

"No," answered Anna. "Just a friend."

As she spoke, Miles looked up and saw them. He looked away quickly.

That night Miles came to her apartment. "Did you see me at the restaurant today?"

"Yes, I did." Anna was very unhappy.

"I'm sorry," said Miles. "I like you, but my business is in trouble. I need money. I need money quickly. When your aunt died, I thought you would get money. We would get married. I could use your money, and my business problems would be solved."

"You were dating me for my money!" said Anna.

"No, no. In the beginning it was just normal. I liked you. But now everything's changed. I need a girlfriend with money. A wife with money would be better."

"Who was the young girl in the restaurant today?" asked Anna.

"Her father owns a glass factory. I hope she likes me. I hope she will ask her father to help me. Please understand. I will lose everything if I don't get some money soon. If I can get the money, maybe you and I can get back together?"

Anna was very angry. She thought about Elizabeth. Elizabeth had asked Anna to forgive her, and Anna had said 'no'.

Anna had thought Miles loved her, but now he was planning to cheat on a very young, girl!

"Just go, Miles," said Anna. "Don't come back."

She thought Miles would change his mind. She thought Miles would say he was sorry. She thought he would say 'It was all a mistake. The money doesn't matter.' But Miles didn't say anything. He walked out of the apartment.

6. NEWS FROM GENEVA

The next few weeks were difficult for Anna. She had loved her job, but now she thought it was boring. When she went home after work, her apartment felt very cold and empty. *I told Elizabeth I had a very good life. What is wrong with me? Why don't I like my life anymore?*

One day, there was a letter in her mailbox. It was from Geneva. It was a big heavy envelope. Inside were two smaller envelopes. One envelope had the name 'Ayesha' written on it. The other one was a business letter. Anna opened it first. It was a letter from a lawyer called Martin Dettwiler. His letter said Elizabeth was dead. She had left half her money to Anna. There was a piece of paper with the letter. It was a list of Elizabeth's money. It was a lot of money. More money than Anna could dream of. *And half of this is mine?* thought Anna. I can't believe it!

Martin Dettwiler's letter said that Anna did not have to travel to Geneva. If Anna sent details of her bank account to Martin Dettwiler, he would send the money to her. The letter said he had also sent a small box to Anna by parcel post.

The end of Martin Dettwiler's letter said ---*I am very sorry for your loss. Elizabeth was a very private person. She never talked about her life, but I was her good friend for many years, so I know you are her daughter. She never stopped thinking about you. My heart is broken because such a special person has died. She was a very strong woman. She helped to save many lives. She had a very hard life, but she never stopped helping other people. She gave me a letter to send to you.---*

Anna's hands were shaking. She put the letter from the lawyer, and the envelope with 'Ayesha' written on it, on the table. She went to the kitchen and made a cup of tea. She came back and stared at the second envelope. She didn't want to open it.

She asked me to understand. She asked me to forgive her. I didn't. And now she's dead. This lawyer in Geneva wrote that she was wonderful. She didn't do anything for me, because she was too busy saving other people.

The telephone rang. It was Miles. "Anna! Sweetheart! How are you? I have been missing you so much."

"I'm fine, Miles. How are you?"

"I'm lonely. I only dated the girl you saw in the restaurant to get some money. I wanted the money for us, so that we could be together. Have you forgiven me? I still love you."

Anna looked at the letter from Martin Dettwiler. *I have a lot of money now. I could give some to Miles. His problems would be over. I'm lonely. I'd like to have a boyfriend again. Miles is weak, but he's fun. And he says he loves me.*

"Anna! Anna! Are you there? Why won't you talk to me?" Miles was talking again.

"So you're still in trouble, Miles. It didn't work out with that girl?"

"No it didn't. But it didn't mean anything. Tell me you forgive me. You are a wonderful girl. Can you give me a little money? Do you have any savings? Did you get the money from the auction? A few hundred pounds would help."

Anna looked at the unopened envelope on the table - the letter from Elizabeth.

What would my mother do? she asked herself.

Anna could hear Elizabeth's voice in her head. She smiled.

"Go to hell, Miles!" she said and ended the call. She switched her phone off. She didn't want Miles to call back.

She felt good. *I'm stronger than I thought.*

Anna sat down at the table and opened the letter from Elizabeth.

7. ELIZABETH'S LETTER

My dearest daughter,

I know it will be hard for you to believe that I love you very much, but it's true. Martin promised me he would send this letter to you. So if you are reading it, you will know that I am dead.

There were some things I didn't tell you the day we met. I must tell you everything now, before it's too late.

The first is that, when we met I knew that I would die soon. I have a brain tumour. There is nothing that can be done to treat it. I will live a little longer, perhaps two or three weeks. It is not enough time. There were so many things I wanted to do.

The second is that I told you that, when you were born, I didn't know your father's real name. This was true, but about three years ago, I saw his picture in the newspapers. I hadn't seen him for more than thirty years, but I knew his face. His real name is James Winchester. The newspapers said he is a retired diplomat. He was being hunted all over Europe because many people believed he was working with terrorists. That was not true. It seems he is a hero.

I worked for the United Nations, and other international groups, for many years, so I know many useful people. I asked questions. He was a diplomat for a long time. Before he was a diplomat, he was a secret agent. That was why he was in Cambodia. That was why he was using the false name, 'Peter Bridges'. Now he lives near a small village in Scotland. The name of the village is Beautore, and he lives in a house called Hill House.

The last thing I have to tell you is very difficult. In 1992, I met a doctor in Algeria. We were working together on an aid programme. We fell in love and we got married. I was forty years old, but we were delighted when I got pregnant. He was killed by a car bomb two months before our daughter was born. So you have a sister. Her name is Miriam. I wanted to keep helping people, but I did not want to give up another child. I had lost you, and I did not want to lose Miriam. I took her everywhere with me. It was easier, because I was more senior, and didn't go into war zones so much. I took management jobs so I could keep her with me. She always had nurses and nannies to look after her. But the places where I worked were still dangerous. She went missing during the Kosovo war. I haven't seen her since 1996. I had left Miriam and her nurse in a Muslim village. The village was destroyed, and it seemed that everyone was killed. For many years, I believed that Miriam had died. Then two months ago, I got some information that gave me hope. Some people from the village escaped into Albania. I don't know if Miriam was with them, but I wanted to go and try to find her. Now it is impossible. I have no time left. I am hoping that you will try to find your sister. I have no right to ask this. But I am not asking for myself. I am asking for Miriam. My lawyer, Martin Dettwiler, will send you all the information I have gathered. Please look at it. It is your choice whether you try to find your sister or not. You are free to choose. But if you do decide to look for her, I think you should ask your father, James Winchester, to help you. He is not Miriam's father, but I remember that he was a very kind man. My contacts here in Geneva tell me that he is also very clever. He will know a lot of very useful people.

Finally, I worked for almost forty years and I never spent much. So I have quite a lot of money. I want you to have half of it. I have left the other half to Miriam. If she cannot be found, or if she is dead, the money will come to you.

Money doesn't make up for the fact that I left you with Maggie, and went off to do what I wanted to do, but I want you to have it anyway. I hope you can use some of it to have fun. Enjoying life is so important. I had a dream and I followed it. I think I was lucky. In all my life, the only thing I have regretted is that I left you behind.

Be happy, my darling daughter. When I met you, I thought that you hadn't found your dream. I hope you will.

All my love,
Elizabeth

8. ANNA MAKES A CHANGE

The next day, Anna sent her bank account details and email address to Martin Dettwiler in Geneva.

Five days later she got an email on her home computer. Half of Elizabeth's money was in her bank account. She went into work and resigned. "I'm leaving here today," she told her boss.

"You have to tell me a month before you leave," he told her. "If you leave like this, you'll never get another job with this bank."

"I don't care," said Anna. "It's time for a change."

She packed the contents of her desk drawers into a cardboard box, said goodbye to Cynthia, and walked out of the bank.

Next, she went to some real estate agents. They agreed to find someone to rent her apartment. Anna was leaving all her furniture, kitchen items, and everything else in the apartment. "I don't want to spend the time packing it all up," she told the agent.

"OK. If you're sure, I'll find someone like a businessman who will want to take it," said the agent.

Anna went back to the apartment and packed a small suitcase. She put the rest of her clothes and personal items into boxes. She called a storage company. They agreed to come the next day and take the boxes away for her. "How long do you want to store the boxes for?" asked the woman at the storage company. "I don't know," answered Anna.

She hired a rental car. The next morning, she was ready to leave. The storage company came early, and so did the postman. He delivered the box from Geneva. By 11:00am she had delivered the keys to the real estate agent and was on the motorway. Her suitcase was in the boot. On the back seat were her personal computer, the box from Geneva, and a paper bag. The bag contained the photograph album, the school notebooks, and the letters from Martin Dettwiler and Elizabeth.

The car had GPS and Anna had no trouble finding her way to the village of Beautore. She arrived there in the late afternoon. The village was on the edge of a sea loch. It was very small. It had a few houses, a shop, a church, and a hotel. There was a sign with an arrow pointing to parking behind the hotel.

Anna got out of the car. She was stiff and tired. *My father lives somewhere near here,* she thought. *I wonder if he comes to this pub.*

She left everything in the car, and walked around to the front of the hotel. She pushed the main door open, and walked in. She was in the hotel lobby, but it was empty. There was a reception desk with a bell. Anna pushed it.

A very small woman came out of a door at the back of the lobby. "Can I help you?" she asked.

"I was wondering if you have a room for tonight?"

"We have five," smiled the woman. "We don't get many people to stay, but the bar is always busy. Just for one person? Will you want dinner? I'm cooking lamb tonight, and I made a nice beef and barley soup."

Anna shook her head. *This woman seems to talk a lot,* she thought. "Just a room please," she said.

"Of course. But you must eat. If you don't want to eat here, you can go back to Lochgilphead. There's a nice place to eat, just off the main road next to the post office."

"Could I have some soup and bread later?" said Anna.

"Of course. I'll show you your room. I'll give you the best one. It has its own bathroom." Still talking, the woman climbed the stairs at the back of the lobby, and Anna followed her. "I'm Fiona Muir. My husband is Len. You'll meet him if you go into the bar."

The room was very nice. "Thank you," said Anna.

"Just for one night? Are you here on business?"

Anna didn't answer. She didn't know why she was there. She didn't know why she had given up her job and her apartment, and driven up to Scotland.

What have I done? she asked herself. *I must be crazy.*

Fiona didn't seem to notice that Anna had not answered her. "Do you need help with your bags? I can tell Len to bring them up for you."

"No, no. I can do it."

"Why don't you go down and have a nice drink in the bar? You will meet some of the locals."

"I don't drink alcohol," said Anna.

"Well now, neither do I. But you don't have to drink alcohol. You could have a nice soda or a fruit juice. Or I could make you a cup of coffee. We don't have a lounge or a living room for guests, and it will be very quiet for you up here in your room alone."

Anna panicked. *I can't go into the bar! My father might be there. Someone might introduce him. I'm not ready!*

"I'll be fine, thank you. I have a book, and I want to rest."

"You have to eat something."

"You're right," Anna answered. "I should have something. You said you had soup."

"Do you want to eat down in the dining room or up here? I can bring you up a tray if you like."

"Yes please, that would be very nice."

"Dinner will be ready at six thirty. If you change your mind, and want to eat in the dining room or go to the bar, just come down."

Fiona finally went away, and it was quiet. Anna lay down on the bed. She had a headache. She was also very worried. *What have I done?* she asked herself again. *Why am I here? I got the money and I went crazy. I ran away from everything and came here. I don't even know if I want to meet my father! Where am I going to go tomorrow, or the next day? I have nowhere to live.*

She went down to her car, and took out her suitcase and laptop computer. She put the bag and the box from Geneva in the boot. *I don't want to see what Elizabeth sent me. Not yet.*

It was almost 7:00pm when Fiona came to Anna's room with a tray of food. Anna had been lying in the dark.

"Sorry I'm late. We got a group of tourists in. They've got a campervan. It's in the car park. They wanted to eat. But now I've brought you some soup, and a little bit of the lamb." She switched the light on and turned to Anna.

"You remind me of someone. Who is it? It's someone I know very well. Do you have family around here?"

"I've never been here before," said Anna.

"Oh. It's strange. Maybe I am imagining things. Just put the tray outside the door when you've finished. I have to get back to the kitchen. Come down for breakfast anytime you like."

The food was delicious, but Anna didn't eat much. She put the tray outside the door and went to bed.

9. HILL HOUSE

Next morning, very early, Anna carried her suitcase and laptop computer downstairs. She met Len, Fiona's husband in the lobby. He was a very big man. He was quiet. He offered her a cup of coffee in the kitchen. She could hear Fiona talking to someone outside. Anna drank the coffee quickly, thanked Len and paid her bill. She wanted to leave without seeing Fiona. *She thought I looked like someone. If she sees me again, she'll remember who it is. I'll drive up to look at my father's house, and then I'll leave. I'll go to Edinburgh. I've never been there, and I've always wanted to see it. I mustn't panic. I have a lot of money, and I can go anywhere and do anything I want.*

Anna didn't want to ask Len where Hill House was. She was sure he would tell his wife, and then she would remember. Maybe Fiona would tell James Winchester about her.

She went out the kitchen door, drove out of the car park and down to the water. The sea loch looked very peaceful in the early morning. Anna parked by the side of the road and read her book. She hadn't slept well the night before, and she was very tired. After a few minutes, she fell asleep. It was mid-morning when she woke up. A fisherman was fixing nets on the beach. She climbed out of the car and went down to talk to him.

"Excuse me."

The fisherman looked up from his work and smiled.

"Could you tell me how to find Hill House? I heard it was somewhere near here."

"Certainly it is. Follow this road until you come to an old fishing boat. Turn left up the hill and drive about a mile. The house is at the top of the hill. It has a stone fence. You can't miss it."

Anna thanked him and went back to the car.

She had no trouble finding the house. It was big, and surrounded by a large garden. There were no houses nearby. Anna felt uncomfortable. *I thought it would be one of a row of houses. No one would know which one I was looking at. This is embarrassing. If I slow down and anyone sees me, they'll know I'm looking at Hill House. I'll have to drive on.* She drove on a little way and stopped by the side of the road. She looked at the GPS. The road continued for ten miles or more. It was very narrow and winding. There seemed to be no more houses until the road met a bigger road on the other side of the hills.

I'll have to go back. Anna had trouble turning the car, but finally she did it. She drove back slowly. As she passed Hill House, a woman was standing by the gate.

She waved to Anna and walked through the gate and onto the road. Anna stopped the car and opened the window.

"Can I help you?" asked the woman. "I saw you drive up past here, and now you're driving back. Are you lost?"

Anna wondered who the woman was. Anna was embarrassed and it made her feel angry. "No, I'm not lost. This is Hill House, isn't it?"

"Yes, it is," smiled the woman. She was tall and very slim. Her hair was white and beautifully styled. She had tanned skin. She was wearing a soft blue sweater and jeans. Anna felt short, overweight and badly dressed.

"I believe it is James Winchester's house." Anna knew that she sounded rude, but she didn't care.

"Yes. He lives here," answered the woman. "Would you like to speak with him?"

I'm here now, thought Anna. *I can meet my father. Do I want to? I suppose so. Otherwise, why did I come to Scotland?*

"Yes. I would. Where can I park the car?"

"No one comes up this road, so you can park by the side of the road if you like. Or I'll open the gates and you can drive in."

"I'll park on the road," Anna said roughly.

Anna was being very aggressive. *I'm angry with everyone,* she thought. *This man who gave Elizabeth a false name. Maggie, Elizabeth and Miles - I'm angry with all of them. I'm also angry with this woman. She's too beautiful and elegant and charming.*

The woman waited while Anna parked the car close to the stone fence. She opened the gate and Anna walked in. "I'm Sarah," she said. She held out her hand to shake hands, but Anna didn't put her hand out. She knew she should introduce herself, but being angry made her rude.

"I'm James Winchester's daughter," she said very loudly. Anna thought the woman would be shocked, but she just smiled and said, "How nice! Did he know you were coming?"

"No," said Anna.

"Well, it will be a lovely surprise! James will be delighted. Follow me," she said. She started walking through the garden. "James is sitting outside with his newspaper. I was doing some gardening when I heard your car."

Around the side of the house, a man was sitting at a garden table reading a newspaper. He looked up and smiled as Sarah and Anna walked towards him.

"You have a visitor, James. I'll make some coffee." Sarah went through a side door into the house.

The man stood up slowly and held out his hand. "Good morning. What can I do for you?"

Anna stopped and looked at him. Elizabeth said this man was her father. He had the same colour eyes as Anna, but Anna didn't think he looked like her at all.

"What can you do for me? You can tell me why you lied to my mother!" she shouted.

James Winchester looked a little surprised, but he wasn't embarrassed or shocked.

"I lied to your mother? Well please, please sit down and tell me about it. I must see what I can do to fix the problem."

Anna wanted to say 'no'. She wanted to stand and shout at him. Then she thought, *I'm angry with everyone, and I'm shouting at him. But I want to hear the story. If I don't sit down and pretend to be nice, he won't talk to me.*

She sat down at the table. James sat down again and smiled at her. "I can see you are very angry. I am sure you have a good reason. Will you please tell me what I did to make you so angry?"

Anna felt calmer. It was impossible to shout at such a charming man.

"My name is Anna Berryman. A few weeks ago, I found out that the woman I thought was my mother was really my aunt. I met my birth mother and she told me. And now they are both dead. Then, I thought I was going to get married, but my boyfriend broke up with me, because I didn't have enough money. Then I got a lot of money, but I told him to go away! And it's all your fault!"

Anna started crying. James leant across the table and patted her hand.

"Oh dear. You have had a terrible time. I'm pleased you came. I will have to see what I can do to make things right for you. Now, take your time. When you're ready, please tell me how I am part of your story."

Anna was crying into some tissues she had pulled out of her pocket.

"You got my mother pregnant. She tried to find you, but you lied to her. She didn't know your real name. She was alone, so she gave me to her sister. If she had found you, she would have kept me."

Anna knew that this was not true. Elizabeth had told her why she didn't want to keep Anna with her. But Anna wanted James to feel sorry.

Anna looked up. She thought that James Winchester would look very sorry, and very embarrassed, but he was smiling. He looked delighted.

"Elizabeth Berryman!" he said. "You are Elizabeth's daughter!"

"And your daughter too!"

"Yes. This is excellent news. I must tell Sarah! We'll forget about coffee. We need to have something special!"

He stood up again and went into the house. Anna noticed that he couldn't walk well.

I have to stop being so angry and rude, she thought. *I have to listen to his side of the story. And why did I say it was his fault that Elizabeth gave me to Maggie? Elizabeth never said that.*

These people are different. I thought Sarah, whoever she is, would be shocked when I said I was James Winchesters' daughter. But she wasn't. I suppose she is James' housekeeper.

And my father isn't upset or embarrassed. He's pleased to find out that he has a child. He hasn't explained anything. They are not like my grandparents, or Maggie or Miles, or the people in the bank. They would all be embarrassed and shocked. My father and Sarah remind me of Elizabeth.

James came back into the garden, followed by Sarah. She was

carrying a tray with glasses and James was carrying a wine bottle.

They were both smiling. "We must celebrate!" said James. "I have a daughter, and she has come to see me!"

Sarah sat down at the table. James opened the wine and poured it into the glasses.

"I don't drink alcohol," said Anna. "Oh," said James. "Sarah. What else do we have that Anna might like?"

"Would you like orange juice?" Sarah asked Anna.

"Yes please," said Anna.

"I'll get it," said James. He stood up and walked towards the house.

Sarah smiled at Anna. "I am so pleased for James. He is so excited that you have come. You know, he never knew anything about you."

Anna didn't want to talk to Sarah. *I came to see my father,* thought Anna. *Why is she sitting here? It should be only my father and me!*

Sarah didn't say anything more. Anna and Sarah sat in silence.

James came back with the orange juice. "You are going to stay with us, aren't you?" he asked Anna. "I hope so. I want to hear everything about you. I want to know how you found me."

Anna didn't know what to do. When she came to Scotland, she had wanted to find out about her father. When she came to Hill House, her plan was to make James feel very guilty, and very ashamed. She wanted him to say he was sorry. But it wasn't working. James was very pleased. He wasn't sorry. He didn't feel guilty.

Anna looked at him. He was so good looking, and so charming. She liked him. He made her feel special. *I wish that woman would go away,* she thought. *Doesn't she realise this is a very special occasion for my father and me?*

Maybe Sarah understood how Anna was feeling, because she stood up. "Of course Anna is going to stay with us. I will go and get a bedroom ready for her, and start cooking lunch."

10. FATHER AND DAUGHTER

James and Anna talked. James wanted to know everything about her life. He wanted to know how Anna found out that he was her father.

"When I got the letter from the lawyer to say that Elizabeth, my birth mother, had died, I left my job at the bank," Anna told James. "I wanted to do something different. Elizabeth left a letter with the lawyer. She wrote about you. She also asked me to look for my half-sister."

"Elizabeth had another child?" James was interested.

"She's much younger than me. Her father was a doctor. Elizabeth met him in Algeria. They got married and had a daughter. But she went missing in Kosovo during the war."

"That's terrible! And what about her father?" asked James.

"He was killed by a car bomb."

"Poor Elizabeth," said James. "She didn't have a lucky life, did she? But she was an amazing person. So kind, so strong, and she was a great doctor."

He stood up slowly. "It's very sad. We'll talk about Elizabeth later. But now, let me show you the garden."

James was talking about the sea view from the end of the garden when Sarah called out, "Lunch!"

They walked back to the garden table. Sarah had put a bowl of chicken salad and a basket of French bread on the table. There were only two places at the table.

"Aren't you going to eat with us?" asked James.

"No. I think we should have a very special meal tonight. I'll go down to the village. Maybe Fiona will have some venison to give me."

"Fiona?" asked Anna. "That terrible woman at the pub who talks all the time?"

Sarah stared at Anna. "Yes, Fiona," she answered quietly. "She is a very nice woman and my good friend." Sarah went back into the house. There was an uncomfortable silence. Then James said, "Let's eat. It looks delicious. Sarah is a very good cook."

After lunch, they went inside, and James made coffee. "We'll drink it in my office," he said. His office was beautiful. There were leather chairs, antique furniture and dark Persian rugs on the floor. The double glass doors opened onto the garden.

"What an amazing room," said Anna.

James smiled. "I like it. I had this furniture in my apartment in Rome."

They sat opposite each other at a low coffee table and drank their coffee. "Do you want to talk about looking for your sister?" asked James. "Perhaps I can help you?"

"Elizabeth put all the information she had in a box," answered Anna. "The lawyer sent it to me. It's in the car. I haven't opened it yet."

"Well, let's go and get it," said James. "We can get your luggage at the same time."

They carried everything into the house. James dropped Anna's suitcase at the bottom of the stairs. "I don't know what room Sarah chose for you. She will take you up later and show you."

They took everything else into the office. Anna put the box on the coffee table and sat down. She looked at the box. She didn't want to open it.

"Shall I open it?" asked James.

Anna nodded.

The box was closed with tape. James went to a desk drawer and took out a knife. He cut the tape and turned the box towards Anna, so she could see what was in it.

On the top was a sheet of paper.

Elizabeth had written---*If you have opened the box, then you plan to look for your half-sister Miriam. I told you to ask your father, James Winchester, to help you. I hope you will go to visit him. If you do, please give him my letter.---*

Anna lifted the paper, and saw an envelope addressed to James. She gave it to him. James took the envelope. He stood up, and went across to the glass doors to open the envelope and read the letter. It was long. When he finished reading, he put the letter in his pocket.

He came back to the table and sat down. "Let's see what Elizabeth found out about Miriam."

11. THE BOX

There was not much in the box. There were photographs - Elizabeth with a smiling man, a baby, and a little girl. There was a marriage certificate for Carim Aldaman and Elizabeth Berryman, a birth certificate for Miriam Margaret Berryman, and a passport in the same name. There were copies of identity papers for Majlinda Luan Gegaj.

"I guess that was Miriam's nurse," said James.

Then there were maps. Elizabeth had marked the location of the village where Miriam and her nurse had been living. There were other maps with circles around the names of towns and question marks. There was a small box with two wedding rings and an engagement ring.

James looked at all the papers very carefully. Then he asked, "Anna, do you want to find your sister? Do you want to look for her?"

"Why do you ask me that?" Anna was surprised.

James was serious. "Your sister might be dead. You will be looking into the past. Sometimes we don't like what we find there."

"I want to look for my sister. Of course I do!" said Anna.

"OK," said James. "Then I will help you. I know a lot of people. I can ask them for information. When do you want to start?"

"Now," said Anna. "I have no job, and no home. It is a good time to look for Miriam. I want to find her as soon as possible."

"Well then, you will want to do some research on the Internet. We will connect your laptop to the WI-FI. I will find somewhere for you to work."

"I will work in here with you," said Anna.

"But there is only one desk," answered James. "If we want to gather information quickly, I must make many telephone calls and send emails. We will find you somewhere else in the house."

"I saw a desk in the room next to this one. Maybe I can work there?"

"That's our living room, but it's Sarah's work room too. Perhaps you can work at the table in the dining room."

Anna was angry. *But Sarah has the kitchen!*

"Why does she need a work room?" she asked.

"Sarah writes children's books. She has worked at that desk for many years."

"But this is your home!" Anna wanted Sarah's workspace. It was a competition. She wanted to win it. "You can tell her to give me her workspace. Sarah won't mind."

James stood up and walked to the wide windows. He stared at the garden. "Maybe Sarah wouldn't mind, but this is not my house. It's Sarah's. It belonged to her grandfather. I came to live here after Sarah and I got married. But even if it were my house, I would never ask Sarah to give up her workspace."

Anna was shocked. *Sarah isn't the housekeeper! She's James' wife!*

"I understand," she said quietly. "Of course the living room will be fine." Anna was very polite, but she was thinking, *He didn't marry my mother. He married this woman. I don't hate him — he is my father, but I hate her.*

James turned back from the window. He smiled. "We'll look for some of the places on Elizabeth's maps on Google. Sarah will be back soon. She will help us set up a place for your computer."

A few minutes later, Sarah came into James' office. "I see you are busy," she said. "But would you like some coffee?"

"Yes please," answered James. Sarah went out and soon returned with a tray of coffee and homemade cake.

She put it down on the low table, and walked back towards the door. "Sarah!" said James. "Please have coffee with us."

"No. Not now. I got some fine venison from Fiona and I am going to prepare a feast for tonight."

12. RESEARCH

The next three days passed quietly. Anna worked in the dining room. "You can have the dining room to yourself. We can eat in the kitchen," said Sarah. James asked Anna to find out about Miriam's father. He asked her to find information about the village where Miriam and her nurse had been living during the Kosovo war. She also looked for stories about people escaping from Kosovo into Albania.

Every day, James went to his office after breakfast. Anna didn't know what he did there, but it seemed he made many telephone calls. Anna could hear him talking and laughing, but she couldn't understand what he said. Sometimes she thought he wasn't speaking in English.

Sarah served breakfast, cleaned the house, and worked at her desk in the living room. James helped with the cooking, served drinks, and washed dishes, but Anna didn't do anything.

I'm busy, she thought. *Sarah's not doing anything to help James and me. Why should I help her?*

Each day, after lunch, Sarah worked in the garden. Anna and James sat in his office, and Anna told him what she had found on the Internet.

Anna found reports of a Syrian doctor who had been killed by the car bomb in Algeria in 1993. The aid organisation gave her contact details for his family. They had moved to Canada in the late 1980s.

James called the family in Montreal. "His brother didn't know anything about Carim's marriage to Elizabeth, or anything about the daughter. He says the family are very excited," James told Anna. "If Miriam is alive, they want to meet her as soon as possible."

James never said anything about what he was doing, or what he had found out. When Anna asked him, he just smiled and said, "I am finding the right people, but progress is slow."

On the third day, while they were eating lunch, James was very cheerful. "I have done as much as I can here, so it's time for stage two! We can start tomorrow, or the day after. I think I'll work in the garden with you this afternoon, Sarah."

"What's stage two?" asked Anna. "You never tell me anything."

James laughed. "I'm sorry. It's a bad habit. Diplomats talk about the weather and sport and restaurants. They never want to give information. Secret agents are worse – they never talk about anything!"

He stood up from the table and smiled at Anna and Sarah.

"Let's go down to the pub for dinner tonight."

Anna didn't want to go to the pub, but she couldn't think of an excuse.

The dining room was almost empty, and Fiona served them a delicious meal.

James introduced Anna to Fiona and Len as his daughter. Fiona stared at Anna, but she didn't say anything. Anna was glad.

It was late when they got back to Hill House. James lay on the bed watching Sarah take off her make-up and jewellery. He sighed. Sarah turned her head. "Is your leg painful?" she asked.

"It's always painful at the end of the day. And maybe I was too energetic this afternoon. I've made good progress. I've found someone who knows the area of northern Albania where some of the people from the Kosovo village may have gone. But there is no one there now who is using the name Majlinda Luan Gegaj."

"Many people who escaped from Kosovo went back after the war was over," said Sarah. "Maybe if the nurse escaped with Miriam, they went back to Kosovo later."

"I can't find any record of a return. If Miriam and her nurse survived the killings in Kosovo, escaped to Albania and went back later, why didn't the nurse contact Elizabeth? No, if they escaped, they are still somewhere in Albania."

"And that's good news?" asked Sarah.

"Maybe," answered James. "Some of the people who escaped

from Kosovo into Albania stopped near the border for a while. Then they travelled to other areas where they had history, or family connections. I have found some family connections to the nurse. They live in small villages in the north. I think that will be the best place to start."

"You didn't find any records for Miriam Aldaman or Miriam Berryman?"

"No. I didn't expect to. I'm sure if Miriam and her nurse escaped into Albania, the nurse changed the child's name. It would have been easier. She wouldn't have to answer questions about the child. I have done as much as I can from here in Scotland. I think we should go to Greece. It's close to Albania, and I can go there to talk to people. We will leave in two or three days. When I know where to look for Miriam, we will go to Albania together."

Sarah didn't answer. She brushed her hair. Finally, she said, "I'm not coming to Greece with you."

"What!" James was shocked.

"I'm not coming to Greece with you."

"Sarah! Why not?"

"Anna doesn't like me. That's OK. I understand. But it will be better if you go to Greece without me."

"Of course Anna likes you! I don't understand what you're saying!" James was very upset.

Sarah turned around on her dressing table stool, and faced James.

"Anna's life was turned upside down. She found out that, all her life, her family had lied to her. Then she and her boyfriend broke up. She is very unhappy and angry. She wants to blame someone. It is easy for her to blame me for everything that went wrong."

James was very surprised. "I can't believe it! It's crazy! It has nothing to do with you."

Sarah laughed. "Yes, I know it's crazy. But that's what Anna wants to believe. She wants time with you alone. Take her to Greece. Go without me."

James got off the bed slowly. His leg was very painful. He walked across the bedroom to Sarah and put his arms around her. "We fell in love when we were very young. We spent most of our lives apart. The day we got married, I promised you that we would never be apart again."

"I know," said Sarah. "That is what I want too. But we didn't know you had a daughter. It changes things. Anna is so angry and so sad. Give her this. I will come to Greece when you know where to find Miriam. I will come when you take Anna to meet her sister."

"So you will come to Albania?"

Sarah laughed again. "Of course! I'll go to Italy and stay with Andy for a while. I guess you plan to ask him to go to Albania with us."

"Yes," said James. "You know me very well. I want Andy to come with us if he can."

Sarah stood up. "I am sure Andy will want to come with us. So Andy and I will meet you and Anna in Greece, and we'll go to Albania together."

13. GREECE

The next morning at breakfast, James told Anna about his plan.

"We can't do any more searching here. We have to go to Albania. It will be easier to plan our search in Albania from Greece, so we will go there first."

Anna was shocked. *I thought James would use his connections and find her. Then I could send her an air ticket. I didn't think that I would have to travel!*

James was still talking. "There is no record of anyone called Miriam Aldaman or Miriam Berryman. My connections couldn't find any record of the nurse either. So maybe they didn't escape the killings, or maybe they are living in Albania using different names. The only way to find out is to go there. We'll go to my house in Greece first. You'll love it. It is on the coast, and we can swim in the sea."

Everything was happening too quickly for Anna. "I don't have any clothes to wear in Greece. All my clothes are in storage."

"You can take your rental car back to Oban today. You won't be using it. You can buy some clothes while you're there." James thought everything was easy. "Why don't you invite Sarah? She loves shopping for clothes."

"No!" said Anna loudly. "I can choose my own clothes! I don't need her!"

James was surprised. *Sarah's right,* he thought. *There is a problem. Why is Anna jealous of Sarah?*

"No problem," he said to Anna. "Maybe Sarah will be busy today. Drive your rental car to Oban, and return it to the car rental company. I'll come to Oban and meet you. We will find somewhere nice for lunch."

Anna left soon after breakfast. She took the car back to the rental car company and went shopping. *I don't know what to buy,* she thought. *I've only been abroad once before, and I was at school then.*

She went to a clothing store and found jeans, shorts, some T-shirts and a swimsuit.

When she went to the counter to pay, the sales assistant was very friendly. "Are you going on holiday?" she asked.

"Yes. I'm going to Greece," said Anna.

"You're so lucky," smiled the sales assistant.

She looked at Anna and then she looked at the clothes. "Please don't think I'm rude, but these colours are not good for you. Browns and oranges are not very exciting, especially in Greece. You will get a great suntan. Why not get the same things, but in blue and pink?"

"No, thank you," said Anna firmly. "These are fine."

She paid for the clothes and left the shop. She was angry. *That woman was so rude! If I chose blue and pink, Sarah would think I was copying her style.*

James took Anna for lunch at a seafood restaurant before they drove back to Hill House.

The next day, Anna and James went to Greece. When Anna went to Belgium with her school class, she had hated it. Everything was different and strange. She never went abroad again. But she loved travelling with James. Everything was so easy. They travelled business class. There were delicious meals, smiling waiters and limousines.

James' house was on the Ionian Coast. It was a long low house above the sea. A husband and wife lived in a small cottage behind the house. "When I built this house, I bought the land from an elderly couple," James explained. "They stayed in their cottage, and I paid them to look after the house when I was away. They cooked and cleaned for me, when I was here. Now their son and his wife do the same thing. Their names are Aretha and Basil. They have a fishing boat and they grow olives."

The time in Greece passed quickly. It was a beautiful and romantic house. The sun shone every day. Anna felt like she was living in a movie.

Sometimes, James disappeared. He never said where he was going, or what he was doing, but Anna didn't care.

She sat on the terrace and read books from James' library. Every day she swam in the sea. She walked into the tiny village and drank coffee at the only café. Everyone smiled at her, and she smiled back.

Aretha cooked all the meals. Anna ate fish, tomatoes, olives and delicious salads. At first she thought the food was strange, but soon she loved it. Everything tasted fresh.

She lost weight. Her skin looked better, and her hair was shiny.

Then one evening, James appeared at dinnertime. He was tired, but he was also very pleased.

14. ALBANIA

"Success!" he said. "I have been talking to some strange people. When the situation was very bad in Albania, these people belonged to anti-government groups. It was a long time ago, but they still have many secrets. They don't like talking about the past, and they don't like talking to strangers. But I think I know where the nurse took Miriam.

"Majlinda came from Elbasan. It is one of the smallest cities in Albania. I found her family. They didn't want to talk to me, but finally her brother told me that she came back to Albania with a little girl. She wouldn't tell her family anything about the child. The family was very angry. They thought the child was hers. They would not let her live with them, so she took the child and went away. There were other family members who lived in the mountains, far from any city. Her brother thinks she went there.

"So we will go to the biggest village in that area. We will stay there and search for Miriam. I have a friend who has found a house for us. He will meet us in the village and translate for us."

"Albania? Why are we going to Albania?"

James was surprised. "Don't you want to find your half-sister? Sarah and Andy will come from Italy. We will go to Albania together.

"Who's Andy?"

"Andy is my nephew. Sarah and I like him a lot. He works at a university in Italy. Sarah is staying with him."

"Why does he have to come?"

"I am old, and my leg is a problem. It is hard for me to drive for a long time. Andy is young and strong. He can drive on difficult mountain roads. We will need his help."

"OK. But why does Sarah have to come?"

For the first time Anna saw James look angry. "Sarah is the love of my life. I want her to go with us."

"I'm going to bed." Anna got up from the table and went to her room.

Sitting at the table, James heard the door close loudly.

He sighed. *Anna is my daughter. I want to love her, but she is so difficult. I am doing this for her, but I am also doing it for Elizabeth. She was such a strong and wonderful woman. She gave so much to so many people. Sarah understands, but Anna doesn't seem to understand anything.*

Sarah and Andy arrived the next day. The back of the Land Cruiser was filled with boxes and packages.

Anna was surprised when she saw Andy. He was tall and handsome. He was very relaxed. He smiled a lot.

"I've got everything you asked for," he said to James. "And other things that Sarah and I thought might be useful."

He hugged Anna. "A cousin! It's wonderful! We'll find your sister, and I'll have a half-cousin too! James is amazing. Every time I think there will be no more surprises from the old man, he invites me on a new adventure! When do we leave?"

The next morning, they left James' beautiful house on the coast of the Ionian Sea. Andy drove and James directed him. They drove for 10 hours. In the beginning, the roads were narrow, but easy. The scenery was wonderful. Then they drove on motorways for a short time. They crossed the border into Albania. There were wide roads and motorways, but James told Andy to take small, empty back roads.

The trip was very difficult for Anna. The roads had sharp corners and were dusty. Anna thought it would never end.

"Why are we driving on these back roads?" Andy asked James.

"I want to meet a friend. He has some things for me. Albania is a modern country, but I want to be careful," said James.

Finally, James said, "Stop here." He looked at his watch. "Good! We are on time."

Andy stopped the jeep on the side of a mountain road. James got out of the Land Cruiser. A man appeared from behind a rock. Anna watched them. The man hugged James and kissed him. They talked for a while. The man gave James a long parcel and went away.

James put the parcel in the back of the Land Cruiser and got back into the passenger seat.

"Do we need them?" asked Sarah.

"Maybe not, but I want to be prepared. It was better to get them here, than to bring our own across the border. We want to find Miriam, but maybe she does not want us to find her."

"OK," said Sarah. "You are not telling me everything you know!"

James laughed. "No, I'm not saying anything, because I'm not sure. But if Miriam is still alive, there must be a reason why she or her nurse never tried to contact anyone in Miriam's family."

Anna was angry. *What is 'them'?* she thought. *What is in that parcel? James, Sarah and Andy are a secret society. I am an outsider.*

"Where do I go now?" asked Andy.

"Drive on," said James. "I'll tell you where to go."

An hour later, Andy drove up a hill. There was a man standing outside a house. He waved. Andy stopped the Land Cruiser. The house was made of stones and seemed to grow out of the ground. It had two storeys and a balcony around the top storey. It wasn't like any house Anna had seen before.

Anna watched while the man, Sarah, Andy and James took everything out of the jeep and carried it into the house. The mystery parcel was taken upstairs, but then she saw a guitar case. "What's that for?" she asked Andy.

"It's mine," he laughed. "I know about these adventures with James. We will spend a lot of time waiting. I will be bored. I have an Albanian-English dictionary too. I will play my guitar and learn a new language until the action starts!"

The first night, they ate food from cans. The meal was cold, because no one could get the old stove to work.

After three days, Anna was going crazy. Nothing was happening. She hated the house. It was dark. They had sleeping bags and slept on old rusty iron beds. The man, his name was Vjosa, stayed with them She didn't like him. His English was perfect, but she thought he was strange.

Sarah cooked and cleaned and read books. Andy played the guitar and studied Albanian with Vjosa. James spent hours talking to Vjosa and sometimes they went out together.

The local people were very nice. They smiled and waved. Every morning there were presents at the door of the house - tomatoes, homemade cheese, eggs, peppers and fresh bread.

On the morning of the fourth day, Anna decided to go for a walk. *If I tell them I am going out, they will want to come with me. Or they will tell me not to go.*

She waited until everyone was busy, and then she went down to the village.

15. WHICH ONE IS MIRIAM?

At lunchtime, Sarah went into the kitchen. "James," she said. "Where is Anna?"

"Isn't she upstairs?" asked James.

"No. She is not in the house. I can't find Vjosa either."

"That's OK. We finally found someone who will talk, but he will only talk to Vjosa. I hope he will come back with news. But where is Anna? Where has she gone? We'll have to find her." James was worried.

He picked up his jacket and called out. "Andy! Anna is out somewhere. We must find her."

Andy ran down the stairs. "OK. What does she think she's doing?"

But as Andy and James went to the door, Anna came in. She was smiling and excited.

"I got tired of waiting for news of Miriam! But it's OK! I have a great plan!"

"Let's sit down," said James. "We were worried about you. What is your plan?"

They sat down at the table in the kitchen and waited for Anna to speak.

Anna was very pleased and very proud. "I went down to the village. There is a shop there. I sat outside, and a woman came and spoke to me. She spoke English very well. She asked me why we came to this village.

"I told her everything. I said we were looking for my sister. I said her name was Miriam Aldaman. I said Miriam would get a lot of money if she came to this house. The woman said the easiest way would be to use the Internet, but there is no connection in this area. So she will make a poster asking Miriam to come here. When she comes, we can take her back to England! It's easy. We won't have to stay in this horrible house. I can go home with my sister."

No one said anything. They all stared at Anna. Then Sarah said, "Anna. Did you give this woman any money?"

Anna was surprised. "Yes of course. I said I wanted her to do it very quickly. She said it would cost a lot of money to make the posters, and to pay people to put them up around the area. I gave her all the money that I had. So our problem is solved!"

Andy put his head in his hands. "Oh Anna. Our problem is now much bigger!"

Anna was very angry. "We have been sitting in this house for days. You were not making progress. I fixed the problem and you are not happy!"

Sarah stood up. "We can't worry about it now. Let's eat lunch." They ate canned meat with bread and tomatoes that someone from the village had left at their door. Sarah made coffee. Everyone sat at the table and waited.

It was late in the afternoon when Anna heard someone walking up to the house. She was happy. "That might be Miriam," she said.

She went to open the door. James stopped her. "Don't!" He locked the door and said, "Come upstairs. We will look from the balcony." Anna didn't understand, but James sounded angry. So she went with James.

Sarah and Andy followed them upstairs to the balcony. They looked down at the road. There were many people standing outside the house.

"Miriam's friends are happy for her," said Anna. "Look! They have come to say 'goodbye' to her."

"Which one is Miriam?" asked Andy quietly.

Anna looked. There were many people on the road and outside the house. But they were not together. There was a young woman in every group of people. They were looking at the house and pointing to their young woman. They were shouting.

"What are they saying?" she asked Andy.

"They are shouting, 'This is Miriam'. But they are all pointing at different women."

"I don't understand," said Anna. "Which one is Miriam?"

"Miriam is not here," said James sadly. "You gave money to the woman you met in the village. You said if Miriam came to this house, she would get a lot of money. So the woman said to people, 'Go to the house where the foreigners are. They have a lot of money. If you take your daughter, your niece, your granddaughter there, maybe they will believe it is Miriam. You will get money, and then you can give some of the money to me.'"

The crowd of people stood outside the house for hours. Many young women came close to the door and shouted. "What are they saying?" asked Anna.

"I only know a little Albanian," said Andy. "But I think they are all saying the same thing. 'I am your sister. Give me money.'"

"I hate these people! They are liars and cheats!" Anna wanted to cry.

James sighed. "No, Anna. They look at us and they think, 'They are rich. They have a lot of money'. You said this. You said if Miriam came to the house we would give her money. Don't judge them. Don't think bad things about them."

When it got dark, the crowd of people outside the house started throwing stones at the house.

It was cold. "Let's go downstairs and eat," said Sarah. "I'm sorry, the menu is the same as at lunch time."

They sat at the table in the kitchen. They could hear people shouting, and the sound of stones hitting the house. Anna didn't say anything. *It's not my fault. No one talks to me. I tried to help, and now everyone is angry with me. It's not fair!*

Suddenly Vjosa came into the kitchen. "Why are those crazy people outside? I had to leave the Land Cruiser in the next valley, and climb over the hill. I came through a window at the back of the house. I know where Miriam is. I think I understand everything."

James looked at Vjosa "Tell me. Tell me what the man told you."

"Everyone in the village knows, but no one talks about it. The man who talked to me is different. He is not afraid.

"There is a group that lives in a hidden place in the mountains. The group says many things. They say traditional Albanian life must be protected. They say that tourists come here and pollute the environment. They do not want foreigners here. They say the money that is given to help Albania will never help the people here.

"The people who live in this village are very kind and friendly. But they are frightened of this secret group. They do not talk about them. They know that they have many guns. So maybe they are terrorists. Maybe some of their members come from other countries. Nobody knows.

"There is a young woman in the group. Maybe she is a leader. They call her Besjana, but I think she is Miriam. The people from this hidden camp heard about the money. Someone will meet us on the mountain road tonight. Maybe Miriam will come. I don't know, but we must hurry."

16. DANGER IN THE NIGHT

James stood up. "Thank you, Vjosa You have done a great job. We will go."

Andy went upstairs. He came back with the mystery parcel. He unwrapped it. Anna saw rifles and bullets.

James looked at Sarah. "Please stay here."

Sarah looked sad, but she said, "OK."

"I'll get my jacket," said Anna.

"No, Anna. You will not come with us. Stay here with Sarah."

In a short time, James, Andy and Vjosa were ready to go. They were carrying rifles.

"Are you going to kill people?" Anna asked James.

"No. I don't want to hurt anyone. But we are going to meet people we don't know, on the side of a mountain in the dark. We don't know if they are environmentalists or terrorists. Maybe they are both. The man Vjosa talked to said, 'They have guns', so we must have guns too.

"We'll go out the back of the house, the crowd of people is still outside the front." They climbed out of the window. James was the last to go. He looked at Sarah. He put out his hand and touched her face. She put her hand against his cheek. Then he was gone.

Anna and Sarah were alone in the kitchen of the old stone house.

"I'll make coffee," said Sarah. She looked tired and old.

The noise outside the house stopped. *I should feel better. I should feel safer. But I don't. It feels dangerous,* thought Anna.

She saw Andy had left a rifle in the corner of the kitchen. She saw

Sarah pick it up.

"Give that to me!" she shouted.

Sarah looked surprised. "Do you want this rifle?"

"Yes. Everything is wrong. Those people outside the house might try to come in. I will have the rifle. They will see the rifle. They will be frightened and go away!"

"Do you know how to use a rifle?" asked Sarah.

"I am sure I know better than you!" shouted Anna. "You are old. My father can't love me, because you are always here. And now I can't meet my sister because I must stay here to protect you. I hate you!"

Sarah gave the rifle to Anna. "I'll go to bed. Please don't shoot anyone."

Anna sat with the rifle for a long time. It was very quiet and very cold. After midnight, she put the rifle in the corner of the kitchen and went to bed.

17. TIME TO FACE THE TRUTH

The next morning, Anna went onto the balcony. It was early and the sky was grey and misty. The house was very quiet. *I'm the only one awake,* she thought. Then she heard someone moving around downstairs. Soon, Andy appeared with two cups of coffee.

He gave one to Anna and they sat in silence, watching the mist.

Finally, Anna said, "Where is everyone? What happened last night?"

"We came back about three am. I guess everyone else is still sleeping."

"But what happened? Did you meet Miriam?"

"I think James should tell you. When everyone is awake, we can talk and make a plan."

"You will make a plan! No one tells me anything. Miriam is my sister, but you won't let me do anything! And I know why! I know whose fault it is!"

"What do you mean?" asked Andy.

It's her," said Anna. "She's always there. I don't like her."

"Sarah?" Andy was shocked. "You don't like Sarah! What has she done to you?"

"She stole James away from my mother!"

Andy laughed. "Oh, Anna. What a fairy story!"

"It's true!"

"It's not true. You are jealous of Sarah. You want to find a reason to hate her. You are like a child."

Anna went to the door of the balcony. "You don't know anything.

You have always had everything. You always had a mother, a father and a family. You don't understand!" she shouted.

Andy took two long steps across the balcony and took hold of Anna's arms. He pulled her over to the table and pushed her into a chair.

He sat down opposite her and held her arms. "Look at me," he said.

Anna raised her eyes and looked into his face. Andy was very, very angry.

"I was so pleased to meet you. I never had a cousin. I thought it would be great. But you are impossible," he said. "I don't care what you do, or what you think. But you will listen to me now.

"Sarah and James met at university. They were very much in love. They planned to marry. James was sent to Cambodia on a secret mission. He thought he would be gone for three weeks. He got trapped in Cambodia. He was there for three years.

"Sarah didn't know where he had gone, or why. She had a very bad time. Her father died, and she was alone. When James came back to find Sarah, she was married to a guy who was crazy."

"James broke my mother's heart," said Anna.

"No he didn't. James showed me the letter your mother wrote to him. She tried to find James, but only because she thought he should know about you. Her heart wasn't broken. She knew what she wanted to do, and the life she planned didn't include James."

"James showed you my mother's letter! That was wrong! That letter was private."

"It was a private letter to James. He can show it to anyone he wants."

Anna was very angry. "So Sarah has seen it too!"

"I'm sure Sarah read Elizabeth's letter," said Andy. "Sarah's and James' lives were very difficult because of the secrets. I'm sure there are no secrets now."

"So why did James show the letter to you and Sarah, and not to me?" asked Anna.

Andy didn't answer. *James didn't show the letter to Anna because he didn't want to hurt her,* he thought. *Elizabeth wrote that Anna wouldn't talk to her. Anna wouldn't listen to Elizabeth, or help her. Now Elizabeth was dead. James worried that Anna might feel bad about it.*

"I don't know," he said.

"No," said Anna spitefully. "You don't know anything. You had an easy life."

"So did you," answered Andy. "You grew up with people who loved you. Your grandparents and your aunt loved you. What was so difficult?"

"Everyone lied to me. All my life people lied to me! Your life is so easy! You wouldn't know what my life was like."

Andy held Anna's arms more tightly. "Wouldn't I?" he asked. "James will never walk properly again, and he is always in pain. That's my fault. I met a girl and fell in love. I got married. Less than twenty-four hours after the wedding, my wife was murdered. James tried to save her. He got shot in the leg, and almost died too. I found out that my love affair and marriage were lies. The woman I married didn't love me. She only wanted money. James was in danger, and she tried to get money from the people who were looking for him. So don't tell me I don't know what it is like to be lied to. At least, the people who lied to you did it because they loved you!"

Andy let go of Anna's arms. They sat in silence on the terrace. Then Anna said, "We don't need Sarah. Why doesn't she go back to Scotland? I couldn't go with you and James to meet Miriam. I had to stay here and protect Sarah. It wasn't fair."

Andy sighed. "Sarah is very good with guns. When she was young, she was a national champion rifle shooter. She is good with handguns too," he said quietly. "James and I wanted Sarah to come with us into the mountains. But she stayed here to protect you."

Anna started to cry. "You all think I am so stupid!" she shouted. She jumped up from the table and ran into the house.

18. THE PLAN

When James and Vjosa came into the kitchen around 10:30am, Sarah was stirring cereal in a pot. Andy was sitting at the table with his Albanian dictionary and a notebook.

"Only food from cans this morning," said Sarah. "We ate all the fresh food yesterday, and there were no presents this morning. I guess the villagers don't like us after all the trouble with the poster."

"Maybe that is not the reason," said Vjosa slowly. "The woman Anna talked to said there is no Internet here. That is not true. Some people have Internet, and many people have mobile phones. I think the people who came yesterday with the fake 'Miriams' came from many different places. I think they were the woman's friends and relatives. I don't think that woman lives in this village. Maybe she was a visitor. Maybe she came from another country.

"There are no presents this morning because everyone in the village knows we talked to people from the hidden camp in the mountains. Now they don't know if we are terrorists. They are frightened."

"How do they know we met those guys on the mountain last night?" asked Andy.

"They know everything that happens. They don't talk about it, but they watch, and they know."

Sarah poured coffee and they all sat at the table.

"Where is Anna?" asked James.

"I think she is in her room," said Sarah. "I haven't seen her today."

Andy was embarrassed. "I don't know if Anna will talk to me again. I was angry with her this morning. She doesn't like you, Sarah. She thinks everyone is against her. I told her she was wrong. I said too much."

"Oh Andy!" Sarah was not happy. "Anna is feeling bad. James and I think we must be kind. It is very difficult for her. What did you tell her?"

"I told her about Cambodia, and I told her about the time when James was hiding because everyone thought he was a traitor. But I didn't say anything about what happened in Scotland, and I didn't tell her about the killer from Cambodia."

James sighed. "I didn't know what to do when my daughter came to Hill House. She had a normal life. We are different people. Our lives were not normal. I hoped she would not hear about my past."

Vjosa banged his coffee cup on the table. "We are doing this for Anna!"

"We are doing this for Elizabeth too," answered James.

"I never knew Elizabeth, but I have watched Anna." said Vjosa. "You are too kind. Tell her to come here, and we will make a plan."

James went upstairs. Sarah, Andy and Vjosa waited. It was a long time before James came down to the kitchen, but Anna came with him. Her eyes were swollen. She didn't look at anyone.

"Last night we went up to the mountains. We waited for a long time. Then some men came from the secret camp. Miriam didn't come," said James.

"The men asked about the money. We told them there was money for Miriam from her mother. We said Miriam's sister was here to meet her. The men said Miriam would come to the same place tonight. So we will all go there, but we must be very careful."

Anna listened, but she didn't talk to anyone or look at anyone. She ate and went back to her bedroom.

It was a long day. Andy played his guitar and studied Albanian with Vjosa. Sarah and James sat on the balcony. They held hands and looked at the mountains.

"Will it go well tonight?" Sarah asked James.

"I don't think it will be good for Anna," he said. "But I can't change reality for her. When we were in Greece I heard about this secret group in the mountains. I thought maybe Miriam was part of this group. But no one had good information. Now we know more.

Maybe Miriam is an eco-warrior. Maybe she is an Albanian patriot, or maybe she is a terrorist. I don't know. But I'm sure Anna won't be happy.

"She is my daughter. But she doesn't understand me, and I don't understand her. I want to find a memory of Elizabeth in her. Or maybe I want to see something of myself…"

Sarah laughed.

"What's funny?" asked James.

"I never met Elizabeth, but I know you! Anna is difficult. You are difficult. Wait and see!"

19. MIRIAM

They left the house when it was dark. Vjosa drove the Land Cruiser. They went up narrow mountain roads. After a while, he stopped. There were thin, sad trees and many rocks.

Is this the place? Anna asked herself. *Is my sister here?*

"About three hundred metres up the road," said James quietly.

Andy and Sarah got out of the Land Cruiser. They were carrying rifles. Andy went to the left, and Sarah went to the right of the road. They disappeared between the trees, then Vjosa drove on up the mountain. He stopped on a corner. They waited in the dark. No one said anything. A truck came down the mountain. It stopped and a man got out. He had a strong, bright torch so they could not see his face.

Vjosa got out and walked towards the light. He came back to the Land Cruiser.

"He says Besjana will talk to the woman with the money."

Anna spoke for the first time. "Who's Besjana? I thought my sister was coming."

"That's what they call your sister. It means 'trust' or 'promise'," said Vjosa. "Get out and walk towards the light."

"It's OK," said James. "Vjosa will go with you, and we will make sure you are safe."

Anna was very frightened, but she got out of the Land Cruiser and walked towards the bright light. Vjosa walked behind her.

She walked past the man with the bright light and saw he had a rifle on his back. Then she saw a woman standing in front of the truck. She was wearing an army uniform. She was very tall and had a lot of black hair. "Are you the woman with the money?" she asked.

She speaks English! Anna was surprised. "Are you my sister?"

"I am the daughter of Elizabeth Berryman and Carim Aldaman. I was called Miriam, but now my name is Besjana."

Anna found it hard to speak, but she said, "I came to find you. I came to help you. You don't have to stay here. You can come back to England with me. I have a nice apartment. We can go shopping. I will help you buy clothes. Maybe you want to go to school."

Miriam laughed. "School! When Majlinda and I came here, she was very angry about the war. She was angry about the troubles in Albania. So she took me to the camp in the mountains. There are many clever people there. They taught me. I speak four languages. How many do you speak?"

"But you will have a better life with me." Anna was confused.

"A better life? An apartment in England? My life is here. I have the mountains and this beautiful country. I have my husband and my people. My husband is a great leader. I want the money from my mother. I want the money to help my people. I don't want you."

Anna's dreams were disappearing. "I'm sorry. I didn't know about you until after our mother died. When I knew, I came to find you. Did you know about me?"

"Yes. Majlinda told me everything. But I wasn't interested. Why would I want an English half-sister? After you came here, I heard about the money. Is there a lot of money? How much is mine?"

I met my mother, but I didn't like her. I didn't talk to her. I didn't help her. I was wrong, thought Anna. *But Miriam isn't interested in Elizabeth, she only wants her money.*

"Our mother was a wonderful person. She helped a lot of people. What about your father's family? They want to meet you. They want to help you too."

Miriam laughed. "Didn't you listen to me? The only thing I know about my father is his name. The woman doctor, Elizabeth, didn't want to be with me. She was too busy saving other people. She left me with Majlinda.

"I had an English mother and a Syrian father, but Majlinda saved my life. If we had stayed in that village near Kosovo, we would have been killed. She was my real mother. My heart is with Majlinda. My heart is in Albania."

I was angry because Maggie and my grandparents lied to me. Miriam has many reasons to be angry too. Elizabeth tried very hard, but now there are two angry daughters. What can I do? Anna asked herself.

"There is a lot of money," said Anna. "Half of it is for you. How can I send it to you?"

Miriam turned her head. Another man came out of the darkness. He didn't speak, but he walked to Anna and gave her a piece of paper.

"That is the number of my bank account in Switzerland. You can send the money to that account."

"You have a bank account in Switzerland?" Anna was very surprised.

"Why not? You think I am a stupid person. I am more international than you. You have a nice apartment in England. You want me to go with you and buy clothes. You want me to be a boring English person! You want me to be like you, but I don't want to be like you."

Anna knew Vjosa was standing behind her. She knew Miriam and the two men from the camp in the hills had guns. They were dangerous people, but she was not afraid. Andy and Sarah had guns too, and they were hiding in the rocks near to the road. *I am safe. Now I understand what James was thinking. James, Sarah, Andy and Vjosa are trying to keep me safe. I didn't understand.*

"OK," she said to Miriam. "You have your life and I have mine. I will tell the lawyer that I found you. I will tell him to send half our mother's money to your bank account in Switzerland. Please use Elizabeth's money well. She wanted to help people. I hope you will use her money to help people, not kill them."

"I will use the money any way I want!"

Anna walked away. She walked back to the Land Cruiser. Vjosa followed her.

They climbed into the Land Cruiser. Vjosa drove down the road a little way, and stopped. After a while, Sarah and Andy appeared out of the shadows and climbed in.

They were almost back at the house when James asked, "Did you hear what Miriam said?"

"Yes," said Vjosa.

"We heard everything too," said Andy.

"What do you think, Anna?" asked James.

Anna didn't say anything.

20. MONEY FOR TERRORISTS?

When they returned to the house, Anna went to her bedroom. The others sat at the kitchen table. James brought out some bottles of local wine.

He was worried. "Tell me what Miriam said. Is Anna OK?" he asked Vjosa.

"Anna did a good thing when she gave that woman money for the posters. The group in the mountains heard about Elizabeth's money. That's why Miriam talked to Anna. Anna promised Miriam half of Elizabeth's money. Miriam is very pleased. She is not interested in Anna. She only wants the money."

"Poor Anna!" said James. "It's sad!"

"No," said Sarah. "It's not sad. Tonight was not good for Anna, but now she understands the truth. She can make her own life."

"Does Anna know that her half-sister might be a terrorist?" asked Andy. "Elizabeth's money might be used for terror attacks."

"I don't think Anna is thinking about that now," Sarah said slowly. "There has been too much drama, but she is not stupid. When she has a chance to calm down and relax, with no secrets and no mysteries, she will understand."

Andy was worried. "But this is wrong! We helped Anna find Miriam. Anna will tell the lawyer to send the money to her. If Miriam is a terrorist, we have helped a terrorist group."

Vjosa and James smiled at each other.

"I would never do that," said James. "Vjosa, tell Sarah and Andy who you are, and why you came here."

Vjosa drank some wine, and said, "I am part of an international anti-terrorism group. James contacted me from Scotland. He asked for advice about how to find Miriam. I was pleased to help. I also told James there were stories about terrorist groups that were in Albania. We believe that these groups have connections to other countries. They are a big threat. They can hide in Albania, and plan attacks in other countries.

"Later, James told me where he thought Majlinda had taken Miriam. I am Albanian. I know my country well. I thought, 'that area would be a perfect place for a secret camp'. James and I made a plan. I came here and found this house. I was the translator for the foreigners who were trying to find a missing woman. No one knew what my real purpose was."

James was happy. "We found Miriam, and Vjosa met some of the people from the camp. Vjosa knows about the group in the mountains now. His organisation will track Elizabeth's money. If Miriam uses Elizabeth's money for the local people, that will be great. If she uses it for new roads, schools and environmental protection we will be very happy. It will be a good way to use Elizabeth's money. But Vjosa will know if any of the money is used for terrorism. We were very clever."

"James!" Sarah was angry. "You never change! You used your daughter to search for terrorists! You should be ashamed!"

"I don't feel ashamed. I promised Anna I would help find her sister. Vjosa was the best person to help us. When he told me that maybe there were international terrorist groups hiding in Albania, I thought maybe we could do two things at the same time. Anna met her sister. OK, it was not a good meeting for Anna, but it was not bad either."

21. ANNA'S FUTURE

Anna woke up early. She lay in her sleeping bag, and looked at the window. The sun was rising, and the room was filled with light.

She thought about many things.

My mother was an amazing woman. She saved many lives. I didn't like my mother when I met her, but I think she made me strong.

My grandparents tried hard to be good parents to me.

I had Maggie. I loved her and she loved me.

My father is so handsome, charming and clever.

I have a cousin. He is a very nice man.

Finally she thought about Sarah. *She makes my father happy.*

She felt different. *All of my thoughts are good thoughts. I feel relaxed. I am another person today. I don't care about the lies and the secrets anymore. And I have enough money to do anything I want!*

Andy woke up. He heard someone moving around in the kitchen. *Coffee!* he thought. *I need coffee.*

He pulled on his jeans and a T-shirt, and went downstairs. He was surprised to find Anna in the kitchen. He stood at the door and watched. There were plates and cups on the table. He could smell coffee, and Anna was cooking something. She was singing.

"Uh, good morning." *This is a different person,* he thought. *She looks happy! It's the first time I have seen her look happy.*

Anna took the pot off the stove. She poured coffee for Andy and sat at the table with him.

"I'm sorry the meeting with your sister didn't go well," he said quietly.

"Did you hear what she said?" asked Anna.

"Yes. I heard everything. You must be disappointed."

"Disappointed?" Anna was puzzled. "I know I should feel bad, but I don't. I have been so angry and unhappy since the day after Maggie's funeral. But today I woke up, and I thought 'I don't care anymore'. I want to forget about everything."

This isn't good, thought Andy. *It's dangerous to try to forget the things that happen in our lives.*

"After my wife was murdered, I tried to forget everything. It was a mistake. I couldn't make a new life, until I understood why the bad things happened. I hope you can do that."

Anna didn't answer, but she smiled at him. *This is the first time I have seen her smile!* thought Andy. *She is a different person when she smiles!*

Sarah, James and Vjosa came into the kitchen about an hour later. They were worried about Anna. Andy was playing his guitar and Anna was singing.

Last night was too much for Anna, thought James. *She is a little crazy today.*

They ate the food that Anna cooked. They worked hard to clean the house, and to put everything back in the Land Cruiser.

Sarah was surprised because Anna helped them. It was almost noon when everything was finished. Vjosa got into the Land Cruiser. "I will leave with you. I want everyone in the village to think I came here as your translator. Then the people in the camp in the mountains will think the same thing."

After they crossed the border between Albania and Greece, Vjosa told Andy to stop the Land Cruiser. A big black limousine was parked by the side of the road. Everyone got out to say goodbye to Vjosa.

He shook hands with Andy, and hugged Sarah and James.

"Until the next time," he said to James.

Then he shook hands with Anna. "Good luck," he said. "I hope you have a good life."

He climbed into the limousine, and it drove away.

Andy drove on towards the Ionian Coast and James said, "Andy must go back to his university in Italy. He has been away too long. What do you want to do, Anna? Sarah and I will go to my house by the sea for a few weeks. Will you come with us? We would like that very much."

"No, thank you." said Anna.

"Do you want to go back to England as soon as possible?"

"No," said Anna.

"But Anna! You must have a plan!" James was worried.

"I have a plan," said Anna. "I have a lot of money from my mother. I woke up this morning and I knew all my problems had gone. Andy said I must not forget the past. I know he is right, but I need time to understand. I know what I want to do."

"What is your plan?" asked Andy.

"I'm not going back to England. I'm not going back to my old life. Elizabeth wanted me to find my dream. I know what my dream is. I like Greece. I'm going to buy a guesthouse. I want a guesthouse with a café or a restaurant. I am going to call the guesthouse 'Sisters'."

THANK YOU

Thank you for reading The Other Sisters. (Word count: 18,741) We hope you enjoyed the story. There are four other books in the Old Secrets – Modern Mysteries series: *The Blue Lace Curtain, End House, On the Run, and Killer.*

If you would like to read more graded readers, please visit our website http://www.italkyoutalk.com

Other Level 4 graded readers include
Birthdays to Remember
Chi-obaa and Friends
Chi-obaa and Her Town
End House (Old Secrets – Modern Mysteries Book 2)
Killer (Old Secrets – Modern Mysteries Book 4)
On the Run (Old Secrets – Modern Mysteries Book 3)
The Blue Lace Curtain (Old Secrets – Modern Mysteries Book 1)
The Legacy
The Temple Treasure
The Witches of Nakashige
Trapped
Vanished Away

ABOUT THE AUTHOR

I Talk You Talk Press is an award-winning Japan-based publisher of language textbooks, graded readers and language learning/teaching resources. We won the Language Learner Literature Award in 2019 and 2020.

Our team is made up of highly experienced language teachers and translators, who have all studied at least one additional language to an advanced level.

This experience enables us to design our materials from the perspective of both the teacher and the learner. We consult with both teachers and language learners when designing our textbooks and graded readers, and test our materials extensively in the classroom before publication.

We are a fast-growing press, and currently publish graded readers for learners of English. We publish new graded readers monthly.